Love Notes

Blueprints for wholesomeness

Kofoworola Toriola

ISBN 978-978-970-938-0
Cover Design: Oluwakemi Oladele

Dedication

To the one true God
The inspiration giver
The ultimate author

To my Dad, Olayiwola Toriola
Thank you for teaching your baby girl to
reach for the stars
You will never get to read this
But I hope the Angels tell you all about
this book

Acknowledgments

Of all my many blessings in life, I am most grateful for the gift of people. I am who I am today because of a strong community of people who are investing in me, constantly rooting for me and cheering me on.

I am immensely grateful to my God for entrusting me with this assignment.

I am grateful to my mum and siblings– my biggest fans. Many thanks to my coach, Mrs. Damilola Adedeji and the entire team at The Birthing Center. To my facilitators at The Fellowship 12 Network, thank you for pouring into this naïve young lady years ago.

To the amazing people that read the first manuscript and watched it undergo series of changes. Your constructive criticism is responsible for this excellent work and I'm grateful – Tope Omotosho, Vera Alex, Olusore Adefioye, Ebunoluwa Ade-Taiwo, Oluwanifemi Obafemi and my coach. To the Book Lady NG, thank you for your professionalism and dedication to excellence.

To my friends, mentioning your names individually will cause problem because I don't want to miss out anyone. From the bottom of my heart, thank you.

Foreword

When Kofoworola reached out to write the foreword for this book, it was a really busy period. I struggled with saying a 'yes'. We had to make compromises to get to this point, but today, I say without a doubt that I am glad I took on this assignment. Kofoworola has bared a bit of her soul in this and it is so great to see how healthy her soul is becoming.

This book is a great starting point for someone who is searching for a blueprint on how to be whole. The simplicity and sincerity of Kofoworola's writing makes it easier to understand and align with. The relatability of the experiences shared also make it easy for so many people to connect with what God is sharing through her.

I am glad to see many more people in this generation taking up the mantle of the prophetic scribes and journaling with the Father. I believe this project will do a work of healing in the heart of those who read it. The encounters detailed in this book are available for everyone, even on much deeper levels. The Lord wants us to have a walk with Him– a deep and vibrant one. A walk devoid of pain, shame, confusion, deceit, anger, etc. God wants to invade you. He wants to give you a name that only He calls you. He wants to show off His goodness with your life as a vocal point.

Foreword

As a result of the plethora of information about our spirituality, it is very easy to fall into error these days. Guard your heart, walk in love, study the word and pursue wholeness so you don't fall for trauma-induced doctrines thinking it is God speaking.

Contrary to popular beliefs, wholesomeness is a journey, not a destination. Everyday on Earth is another journey on the wholesomeness journey. It might be tough; you will want to give up but remember that your destiny is heavily depending on your wholesomeness for the execution of the divine assignments on your life. This manual is a great place to start.

May the Lord help us all!

Ibukunoluwa Akinbamijo
President, The Waiting Brides Network and the Kingdom Men Initiative

Table of contents

Table of contents

Table of contents

Introduction

In my few years of living, certain experiences and learnings have been instrumental in shaping me to become who I am today. In my daily interactions with people from all walks of life, I understand that these experiences are not unique to me. While writing, I had you in mind and it is my utmost desire that as you read, you feel loved and experience the Father's love on every page. I want you to come to an understanding that God is interested in every detail of your life.

These love notes are largely influenced by Newsletters I shared with a close community sometime in 2020. They were birthed from an instruction given by God to write. As you read, you'd find that the writing style is conversational, that is because I am writing as if in a conversation with you.

Please read the love notes prayerfully and purposefully. Read with an intent to be blessed.

Don't just read because I wrote it. Instead, read because God wrote it, and He is speaking to you through it.

I hope you win on this journey called LIFE. If these love notes are a blessing to you, please do not hesitate to recommend to others.

1

"In Him we were also chosen, having been predestined according to the plan of Him who works out everything in conformity with the purpose of His will, in order that we, who were the first to put our hope in Christ, might be for the praise of His glory."
Ephesians 1:11-12

Recently, I started insisting that people call me by my full name "Kòfowórọlá". It is a mouthful so some people do not understand why I don't prefer the shorter form "Kòfo" especially because that is what I had been called for over two decades. Others think I am being dramatic because, in their words "it is just a name" it's no big deal.

Here is the thing, my name is important to me because it ties to who I am and who God has called me to be. My name is synonymous with wealth. Kòfowórolá means "I attract wealth... wealth comes to me naturally" etc. I learnt early that God has called me to be a kingdom financier. Every time I am called my full name, it is a reminder of what God says, regardless of my current reality.

When you ask me who I am, amongst many other things, I will tell you, "I am a Kingdom financier".

Do you know who you are?
Do you know who God calls you?

Take a minute to ponder on this question, "who am I?"

When all your titles are stripped away, "Who are you?"
Beyond the glitz and glamour (job, family name, status, fame, finances etc.), "Who are you?"

I learnt that your identity will be tied to whatever you give your heart to.[i] The Bible says, *"For where your treasure is, there will your heart also be" (Matt 6:21).* Therefore, it is important you guard your heart with

"*Your identity will be tied to whatever you give your heart to*"

all diligence because out of it are the issues of life.

What have you allowed to define/shape you?

What have you allowed to take root in your heart? Hurt, abuse (emotional, physical, mental. etc.), insecurities, rejection, pain, esteem, pride, arrogance *[fill in the blank]*?

Have you been operating in your identity or are you who society has conditioned you to be?

When you find your identity in the One who created you, it will change your whole perspective. Sometimes, God lets you lose your sight so you can see – ironic? He strips you of certain things so you can hold on to what really matters– **Your identity in Him**. It is in Christ that we find out who we are and what we are living for.

THE EPHESIANS IDENTITY CURRICULUM

- You are an expression of God's love - *"And in love He chose us before He laid the foundation of the Universe! Because of His great love, He ordained us, so that we would be seen as Holy in His eye with an unstained innocence" (Eph 1:4 TPT). "...for the same love He has for the Beloved Jesus, He has for us" (Eph 1:6 TPT). "But God still loved us with such great love. He is so rich in compassion and mercy. Even when we were dead and doomed in our many sins, he united us into the very life of Christ and saved us by his wonderful grace" (Eph 2:4-5 TPT)*

- You are a child of God - *"For it was always in His perfect plan to adopt us as His delightful children, through our union with Jesus, the Anointed One, so that His tremendous love that cascades over us would glorify His grace" (Eph 1:5 TPT, Eph 2:19-20 TPT)*
- You are a unique expression of God's divine idea. *"Long before He laid down earth's foundations, He had us in mind..." (Eph 1:3-6 MSG, Eph 2:10 TPT)*
- You are God's expensive purchase, paid for with tears of blood. *"Because of the sacrifice of the Messiah, His blood poured out on the altar of the Cross, we're a free people– free of penalties and punishments chalked up by all our misdeeds" (Eph 1:7 MSG)*
- You are God's poetry. Our lives are the beautiful poetry written by God that will speak forth all that He desires in life. (Eph 2:10 TPT)
- You are God's dwelling place. You are a carrier of the presence of God. You host His presence. *"This entire building is under construction and is continually growing under His supervision until it rises up completed as the holy temple of the Lord himself. This means that God is transforming each one of you into the Holy of Holies, His dwelling place, through the power of the Holy Spirit living in you!" (Eph 2:21-22 TPT)*

If you are ever confused about your identity and who you are, take a deep dive into the book of Ephesians Chapters 1 and 2, therein lies your answer.

2

"So all of us who have had that veil removed can see and reflect the glory of the Lord. And the Lord–who is the Spirit–makes us more and more like Him as we are changed into his glorious image"
2 Corinthians 2:18 (NLT)

Do you struggle with your self-esteem or identity? Have you had to lose yourself to please people?

If your answer is yes, we are in this together. Judging from the previous chapter, you'd probably think that I am so put together and I have this Identity thing figured out. Sorry to burst your bubble, but this is far from the truth. Let me tell you about a season in my life where I struggled with my identity.

A few years ago, I developed a problem that I needed the help of the Holy Spirit to be delivered. I had just received another "you need to go out to start meeting people *ooo*" advice after mentioning my single status. At this point, I had lost count on the number of times I received this particular advice. If people kept giving this advice, it must have been tested and trusted right? Plus, the advice seemed apt because I was really a couch potato – I wore my house like a cloak and lived such a triangular life.

So, the journey began. I started actively trying to meet people. I went out more and took such meticulous care when getting ready. I was on a full operation "I must meet someone and graduate from the school of singleness". The entire process was painful.

First, I had to create this new persona to attract certain kinds of people. I was no longer going out solely because I enjoyed it and truly wanted to have fun. I started going out with the mindset that it's a potential meet and greet and status exchange event. Because of this faulty mindset, I noticed I became overly conscious, I calculated my words and actions. I was basically performing for an audience that could care less while neglecting the most important audience- God and myself.

Did I mention that when I was done performing and unmasked, I felt extremely sad and dejected because the audience I was performing for wasn't buying the act? I beat myself up and began to wonder what was wrong with me. Am I not beautiful enough? Was I not doing enough? I also had instances when I finally met someone who wanted a platonic relationship but because I was already building castles in the air, I got heartbroken due to no fault of the person.

One day I had gone to the mall to buy stuff but more importantly with the mindset of meeting someone. I looked overdressed, but I was team *never to be caught unfresh* because you never know. While shopping for stuff, I was also shopping for the "other stuff".

"Satan has created the false narrative of a scarcity mindset. It is a perception of scarcity that makes us more desperate and anxious"

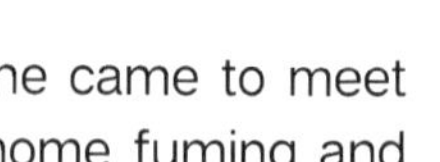

Unfortunately, and fortunately for me, no one came to meet me. I was extremely upset and sad. I got home fuming and wondering what was wrong with me.

Then the Holy Spirit finally had my time and opened my eyes

to what I had reduced myself to. We had a very frank conversation and that's how I got my deliverance. Now when people tell me "When you don't go out to meet people" to rationalize my singleness. I am quick to let them know that I go out to have fun and enjoy myself. I dress to look good to myself. If I meet people as an add on, it is perfect.

The reason why many of us, like me, are going through this kind of experience is that Satan has created the false narrative of a scarcity mindset. He plants seeds of scarcity through people around us and through social media. It is a perception of scarcity that makes us more desperate and anxious. What God really requires from us is trust. Trusting Him enough that He will work things out in our favour. God wants us to know that He is enough for us and that our validation should only come from Him.

3

"The Lord said to Abram after Lot had parted from him, "Look around from where you are, to the north and south, to the east and west. All the land that you see I will give to you and your offspring forever"
Genesis 13:14(NIV)

In law school, I didn't realise early enough that I needed glasses. I just knew that I was struggling to read the presentation slides and I had to rely on my friend's notes. Since I could not see, I just slept. Please don't be like me.

Fast forward to a few months after law school, I decided to get these wonderful eyes of mine checked. After a series of tests, I was handed over a new pair of glasses. Trust me when I say I kept looking outside like someone visiting Lagos from the village for the first time (if you watch old Nollywood movies enough, you'd get the drift). I kept *awwing and oohing*, like the sky is really this bright? the leaves are really green? It was such a revelation that I had to restrain myself from screaming, "I can see!". I am such a drama queen. For the first time in my adulthood, I could see – in HD.

As we approach the end of every year and the beginning of another, the buzz word on the streets of social media is usually something called "Vision Board". A vision board is a collage of images and words representing a person's wishes or goals, intended to serve as inspiration or motivation.[ii]

A vision board, like my glasses, is supposed to help you see your goals clearly. You will agree with me that you can't have a vision board without a vision. It is like buying a car without knowing how to drive, you are going to be stuck in a position. The vision board is the canvas on which your revelation, vision and faith align.

The purpose of this chapter is to give an insight on visioning and the importance of writing it down and making it plain, so that you and anyone that reads it can run with it.[iii]

Visioning starts with revelation, and God is a God of revelation. I pray that the God of our Lord Jesus Christ, the Father of glory, grants you the spirit of wisdom and of revelation - that gives you a deep, personal and intimate insight – into the true knowledge of God, amen.[iv]

A separation activates revelations. After the separation of Abraham from Lot, Abraham received a revelation.[v] Sometimes, the secret to your revelation from God comes from separating yourself from things, places and people. Until you detach yourself from those draining relationships and activities, your vision will continue to be blurry or distorted. Stop holding on to things that you need to walk away from.

Stop trying to fit into that circle when you should be standing out. Stop trying to scramble for a seat at that table when you should be inviting people to sit at your table.

Vision gives you a glimpse of God's future plan for you and gives you an opportunity to structure your life and pray accordingly. A lot of us can't see because our vision looks nothing like our present, it looks like our future

I pray that the Holy Spirit reveals the Lots in your life and gives you the courage to detach yourself from them so that you can receive the revelation required to activate your vision.

According to Cindy Trimm in her book titled *"Hello Tomorrow"*, *"Vision gives you a glimpse of God's future plan for you and gives you an opportunity to structure your life and pray accordingly. A lot of us can't see because our vision looks nothing like our present, it looks like our future"*. When you are a visionary, your today does not dictate your future but your future dictates how you live today. Vision brings illumination and clarity and dispels confusion.

Vision harnesses the power of imagination. I am sure you are familiar with the quote, "if you can dream it, you can achieve it". Whatever you imagine, will emerge. However, the bridge between your imagination and your vision is in the written word. You must be diligent to sit and write your vision.

Why is it important to write down your vision? To make it easy for you and those connected to the fulfilment of that vision to run with it.[vi] Every forward-thinking company has a vision statement which describes the company's goals over a period. I have never read a vision statement written in fine print. It is typically bold enough for everyone – founder, employees, customers, service providers etc. – to read.

Once you activate the power of your vision, you automatically activate your faith. Faith allows you to see what an average person is blinded to. It is the confident assurance that something you want is going to happen. It is the certainty that what you hope for is waiting for you, even though you cannot see it up ahead.[vii] You can run as far as your vision can carry you. “Your feet cannot take you where your vision has never been!”.

The journey from where you are to where you want to go begins with a revelation, your revelation dictates your vision, and your vision is activated by faith.

love notes

4

Un-boxed Christianity

"One Lord, One Faith, One Baptism
One God and Father of all,
who is over all and through all and in all."
Ephesians 4:5-6

For a lawyer, it is very ironic that I do not like rules. I obey them just because, but I detest them all the same. I think it is really because it makes me feel boxed and stifles my ability to express myself. I feel the same about religion and I struggle a lot with "religious" activities.

What is Religion?

"Religion is a burdensome yoke of man-made rules and dead rituals; a futile attempt to please God and save oneself by good works".[viii] There is so much anger in this definition and I would like to agree. Religion is laced with activities, ceremonies, doctrines, rules etc. The devil has offered religion – of rules and regulations – to try to get us to make a never-ending attempt to be good enough to deserve God's blessings.[ix]

I like the way Roy Gustafon tries to differentiate between Religion and the Gospel.

"Religion is man's quest for God; the Gospel is the saviour – God – seeking lost men.
Religion originates on earth; the Gospel originated in heaven.
Religion is man-made; the Gospel is the gift of God.
Religion is the story of what a sinful man tries to do for a holy God; the Gospel is the story of what a holy God has done for sinful men.
Religion is good views; the Gospel is good news"

I dare say that the reason why some of us are still struggling in our Christian faith is most likely because we are religion driven as opposed to God-driven or like someone said we practice "Churchianity" as opposed to "Christianity".

The reason why some of us are still struggling in our Christian faith is most likely because we are religion driven as opposed to God-driven or like someone said we practice "Churchianity" as opposed to "Christianity.

Growing up, we were taught to do things in a certain way to affirm our Christianity, to follow certain rules, such as pray every morning, read your Bible every day, pray in a particular sequence etc.

Many of us were not taught that God is multifaceted and diverse, even in His communication with us. As we began to grow in our Christian faith, this multidimensional God became strange to us because He did not fit the idea of what we were used to as a result of religion, so some of us began to struggle.

Sometimes, we get so beat down because we are failing woefully on the scorecard of religion. I believe the world would be a better place if there were fewer religious people and more God-oriented people. Many of us are so religious we forget how to be Christians – Christ like.

I used to be guilty of this and sometimes I still struggle. So, I stopped putting God in a box. I stopped trying to fit God into the idea of who my limited mind perceived Him to be. I started what I termed "Un-boxed Christianity" – not conforming to the world's standards of Christianity but God's, by the leading of the Holy Spirit.

I am more focused on whether my actions or inactions represent Christ as opposed to the church. Please note that this is not a call to be disobedient to constituted authorities. Rules are important to guide us so we can live orderly. However, the focus should be more on honouring God than trying to get an A on a religious scorecard.

Few years ago, I used to be so beat down when I missed my prayer time in the morning because it was customary to pray every morning. I would be so stuck on the fact that I had missed my prayer window and instead of just praying in the moment, I look for the next best time which might never come. Eventually, I would go the whole day without praying.

On that note, let us try a new approach. Anytime the devil makes you feel guilty for missing a religious routine – e.g. not praying in the morning – silence him by doing exactly what he has accused you of not doing. For instance, instead of moping that you did not pray in the morning, if the devil mocks you by 12 noon that you have not prayed that day, silence him by praying at that very moment. This approach can also be applied to any religious activity. Bear in mind that God that listens to you in the morning, listens to you by 12 noon.

love

5

"We demolish arguments and every pretension that sets itself up against the knowledge of God, and we take captive every thought to make it obedient to Christ."
2 Corinthians 10:5 (NIV)

I was such a sweet child growing up, if I do say so myself. But I had anger issues – hard to believe, right? I had the phone-breaking, PS3-shattering kind of anger. It was difficult to tell because I looked really sweet. My problem was, I bottled up my emotions so much that an outburst was heinous. The worst part was, when I lashed out and needed to explain myself, it was a cry battle. I couldn't make any logical sense because I will be upset and I will be crying at the same time, not a pretty sight to behold, I promise.

I still get angry today- don't let my sweet smile fool you. I get really upset but the difference is, I am mastering the "Doctrine of Tracing".

In Law, there is an equitable doctrine known as "Doctrine of Tracing". It is the process of tracking the ownership of a property or its characteristics from the time of its origin to the present.[x] Don't worry, my intention is not to convert you to a lawyer if you're not one.

In this case, I am not referring to tracking/tracing property but our thoughts. Applying the doctrine of tracing to our thoughts simply means taking a deep dive into our emotions to ascertain the root cause of what and

Applying the doctrine of tracing to our thoughts simply means taking a deep dive into our emotions to ascertain the root cause of what and how we feel each time.

how we feel each time. I have applied this for a while now and found it extremely helpful. I have adopted the "Why" approach– asking Why until I am satisfied.

Have you ever woken up very moody or has your mood ever flipped in the course of the day and you can't seem to place your hands on what triggered it? Yes, I guess. If your answer is no, then you are special – like really special.

Anytime I feel like I am losing grip on my emotions and about to have a breaking moment, especially when I can't seem to pinpoint the cause of my anger, I start an array of self- interrogation. "Why do I feel this way?" "What happened in the course of my day that triggered me?" It could just be that I am just being hormonal, but I won't know if I don't probe myself deeply.

If you don't keep asking the why until you lay hold of the root cause of your emotions, you will be putting a square peg in a round hole. Tracing helps you to properly distil your thoughts and makes it easier to tackle whatever is wrong.

When you finally ascertain the root cause, everything begins to add up and you realise that you are not crazy after all.

I would be lying if I told you that I apply this doctrine in every scenario or even remember to apply it. Although, tracing helps us to ascertain the root cause, we also need to learn how to manage the emotions when they arise.

The very first step is acknowledging that you cannot do it on your own. Joyce Meyers in her book *"Managing Your Emotions"* revealed some truths about managing one's emotions:

- We fight against emotions by using our will to decide to follow God's word rather than our feelings.
- When someone annoys you or does something hurtful, cry out to God, tell him how you feel. He understands because he has been there
- Satan wants us to listen to our feelings which are changeable and unreliable rather than listening to the voice of the Holy Spirit -who always speaks the truth.

There are loads of self-help books and techniques on how to manage our emotions and what to do when we are faced with certain circumstances. You will however agree with me that in the heat of the matter, it is like all the learnings fly out the window. Ultimately, we need the help of God to manage our emotions effectively. If you depend on your own flesh through sheer willpower and determination alone, you will fail every time.

6

FireLighters vs Firefighters

"As iron sharpens iron, so one man sharpens another."
Proverbs 27:17 (NIV)

I am judging you if the first thought that came to your mind when you read the topic were the fine men and women on Station 19. I am also judging you if match sticks were the first thought that came to mind.

Firefighters in simple terms are an energy drainer. They are those friends and even sometimes family around you that quench your fire, weaken your resolve, get you off track etc. They are sometimes well-meaning but their mind is just too small for the vision God has placed in your heart. They tell you to fly, just not too high – intentionally and sometimes unintentionally.

Firelighters on the other hand are your *ginger** brothers and sisters, they *gas** you up to do more, be more, strive harder, work harder and even smarter. They tell you the truth when you mess up so you can be better. They look out for you, connecting you with people that can help you achieve your goals. They are your accountability partners, prayer partners, purpose partners etc.

I am sure you already have a name or two of people who fall into either category in your life. I really hope you have more firelighters. I tell anyone who cares to listen that one of the many blessings in my life is the gift of good and quality relationships – family, friends, mentors, coaches, amongst others. I am indeed blessed in human resources. God is so intentional about the quality of people he places in my life (allow me to brag a little), and I am glad that the majority of them are firelighters.

Firelighters are very important and pivotal to helping you achieve your goals for the year, in life and ultimately, your purpose. They don't always have to be close to you, but they can influence you from a distance. I am sure that at some point in life, you have had a mentor that mentored you from a distance.

In this season, it is important to identify those around you or those you observe from a distance, that are firelighters. If the relationship is already waxing cold, begin to fan the flame. God has not called you to walk alone – just like Liverpool (bad joke) – therefore he puts people in your lives and vice versa to help you achieve your goals.

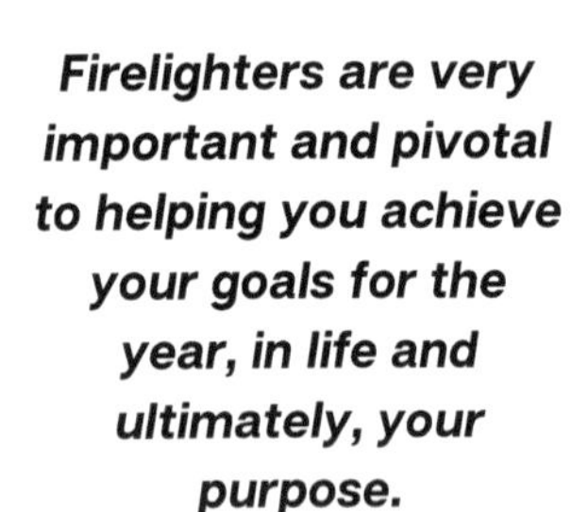

To encourage and keep you focused, look for the firelighters around you. People that will uphold you and ensure that you succeed.

Also, do not be selfish, identify the people you are a firelighter to and strengthen the bond or even do more. Identify the people you are firefighters to, repent and begin to be a firelighter – pass the touch. The world is more beautiful when our flames are burning together.

Don't forget to be the light.

7

"I look up to the mountains; does my help come from there?
My help comes from the Lord, who made heaven and earth!"
Psl 121: 1-2 (NLT)

In 2020, I was in a state of comatose – feeling extremely uninspired and unmotivated for a whole month. Let's just say I had Bruno Mars' "Lazy Song" on repeat.

I did not even achieve my goals in that particular month and the one I managed to achieve was not without a fight. It was a case of money cannot and must not waste. Following my experience in that unproductive month, I decided to take a step back the following month to restrategize.

First, I watered down my goals to just one, unlike the typical four and above goals, I set in a month. Secondly, I decided to seek God's face concerning every aspect of my life. Thirdly, I sought help by reaching out to friends. The third step was out of character, and I am ashamed to admit it. I struggled at first but finally got a hang of it. I am glad to announce that I had better luck with my goals in the following month. *Hallelujah!*

It is interesting that a lot of people– like me – do not like to seek help. This is not a category I am proud to identify with, but I am a work in progress. For some, it stems from a misguided notion that we don't need anyone. By asking for help, I am not referring to monetary assistance – far from it. I mean, if you are faced with a challenge whether in your career, education, marriage, finances (including financial planning), finding purposes etc., there are people around you who have gone through similar experiences and are more than willing to assist. All you need to do is ask – *sọ̀rọ̀ sókè**

Before I got the revelation of this life simple nugget, I

struggled a lot. I was constantly tired and overthinking. Also, things I could have gotten in days took years only to realise later that I actually know someone that knows someone.

Permit me to say that pride is one of the propels of not seeking help. Some of us think asking for help makes us vulnerable or exposes us as weak. Ask yourself. "who am I forming for?". No one really cares about most of the things we worry about. My experience taught me that it is okay to reach out to people and be vulnerable. No man is an island. If human relationships were not important, God would not have seen the need to create Eve. I have found that the Devil thrives in secrecy– whom the devil will kill, he first isolates. He leverages your weakness and strips you of every form of creativity and joy until you do not recognise who you are anymore.

Make a conscious effort today to reach out and to make yourself reachable. The latter is as important as the former. We should be the light that also lights up others (refer to the previous chapter). *"No one lights a lamp and puts it in a place where it will be hidden, or under a bowl. Instead, they put it on its stand, so that those who come in may see the*

light". [xi]

Reach out with wisdom as well. Be intentional about the people in your circle. If you feel like you don't currently have a circle that you can lean on in your unmotivated moments, prayerfully seek out firebrand circles – people that share your God-given purpose and vision. Always leverage your accountability partners.

Asking for help is really helpful (pun intended).

8

"Though he slay me, yet will I hope in Him..."
Job 13:15a (NIV)

I always boast about being God's favourite child, but I will be lying if I told you I have never felt like God has abandoned me or that my prayers were falling on deaf ears. I will be a hypocrite if I told you that God has answered all my prayers such that I have nothing else to pray for except that His

Kingdom comes. We cannot all be like Job, although I aspire to such a level of total surrender. I have gone through certain experiences in life that shook my faith and even made me doubt God. Maybe I have not outrightly said "God does not make sense" but trust me when I say I have had difficult conversations with Him.

In 2017, I was so mad at God that I resolved to stop attending church, praying etc. Basically, I "borrowed" my life back from Him until I was ready to start speaking to Him again. I remember reading the book *"When God does not make Sense – Holding on to your faith during the hardest times"* by James Dobson many years ago where he shared testimonies and trials of faith by children of God. The book exposed me to the understanding that when certain things happen, God is not attacking me personally, He is not out to get me.

The test of faith is part of life. Maybe even a ritual that all Christians must pass through. They are also important to help us build

> ***The test of faith is part of life. Maybe even a ritual that all Christians must pass through. They are also important to help us build character and teach us total dependency on and surrender to God***

character and teach us total dependency on and surrender to God. Our attitude to trials and, tribulations tests whether we believe that God can be trusted. Let me quickly emphasize that **God can be trusted.** God is sovereign and He does as He pleases but if there is one thing I know about God, there is always a bigger picture.

It is important to note that sometimes our delayed testimonies and unanswered prayers are self-inflicted. God entrusts us with certain assignments and tasks at different points in our life. But a lot of the time, we look at other people's clocks instead of focusing on ours and this stalls our growth process. Sometimes God blocks certain opportunities because he needs us to tend our current garden. God's future plan will not show up until we obey His present instructions and our willingness to do what He has called us to do per time is what leads us to answered prayers and ultimately destiny. God is a God of order and precision. With Him, you can't skip steps, you must take things a step at a time.[xii]

He always has a lesson for us at each stage. Our job is to pick our lessons to help us with the next phase. When we try to skip the process, we feel like God is stalling. Remember, when it feels like God is not doing anything, it is not because He does not love you. It does not matter where you are right now or what you think you have done, you are not undeserving of God's love, please remember this.

Go back to the drawing board, ask God what garden He needs you to tend in this season. Then stay there! Rest in the knowledge that God loves you and that everything will work out in your favour. Do your part and trust that God's timing is the best time.

9

"To give to those who mourn in Zion Joy and gladness instead of grief, A song of praise instead of sorrow. They will be like trees that the Lord Himself has planted. They will all do what is right, And God will be praised for what He has done."
Isaiah 61:3 (GNT)

In Secondary School, we sang this popular song during assembly every Monday morning.

"I will clap for the stars of the week
I will clap for the stars of the week

I will like to be a star
For now, I'll clap for the stars"

I sang it by routine then without in-depth understanding. However, a while back, I saw a post where someone said something to the effect; that she will continue to cheer people on regardless of her current standing in life. Immediately, this song came to mind.

Who would have guessed that from a tender age, we were taught to be cheerleaders when others succeed? True to the song, on some days, it was my turn to be clapped for. However, if I never became the star of the week, it would have been perfectly fine. It did not stop me from cheering the stars on. It did not also mean I was not a star in my own right, it just meant that there was something the star was doing better than I was or even maybe not.

As children, we sang that song gleefully and it makes me wonder what happened to us as adults. It is so difficult to practice the lines of the song today. Where did this spirit of bitterness stem from?

Hey! Listen, you are human when you don't feel like clapping for others sometimes. It is life and it is fine. What is not fine is dwelling on that thought such that it takes root in your heart and leads to bitterness.

Ecclesiastes 9:11 comes to mind, "*...The fastest runner does not always win the race, and the strongest warrior does not always win the battle. The wise sometimes go hungry, and the skillful are not necessarily wealthy. And those who are educated don't always lead successful lives. It is all decided by chance, by being in the right place at the right time.*"

You're human when you don't feel like clapping for others sometimes. It is life and it is fine. What is not fine is dwelling on that thought such that it takes root in your heart and leads to bitterness.

On a particular Saturday, about 10 people on my WhatsApp were either getting married or engaged. For a split second, I was extremely jealous, and thought to myself, "*God me nko?**" But the Holy Spirit drew my attention to my feelings, and I immediately repented.

A friend shared something very profound with me on jealousy using the story of Joseph in the bible. He said, "Joseph saw 11 stars bow for his star, but jealously made his brothers forget they were stars too". If Joseph's brothers had the right heart posture, they would have seen that they were not less of a star because theirs was not shining the brightest at that moment. If only Judah, one of Joseph's brothers, knew that his lineage will birth Jesus.

I believe feeling jealous in itself is not bad. However, dwelling on the feeling such that it begins to lead to hatred or resentment is the real issue.

I remixed the song above as follows:

I'll clap for the stars
Of the week, month
Year, decade
I will like to be a star
But for now
I will clap for the stars

Do not stop cheering people on, on your journey. You are not less of a star because yours is not shining the brightest at the moment.

10

"Because of this decision we don't evaluate people by what they have or how they look. We looked at the Messiah that way once and got it all wrong, as you know. We certainly don't look at him that way anymore. Now we look inside, and what we see is that anyone united with the Messiah gets a fresh start, is created new. The old life is gone; a new life emerges! Look at it!"
2 Corinthians 5:15-17 (MSG)

I was having a conversation with a friend, and I just started writing this particular chapter. While conversing, the word EVOLUTION came to mind.

Certainly, not evolution as we know it– the theory of evolution

I.e. from animal to man. For the purpose of this chapter, evolution is defined as the gradual development of something or someone – you and me.

A little back story – my friend and I were reminiscing about our University days when somebody came to mind and my friend tried to draw my attention to his now positive traits. This individual was a notorious "bad boy" when we were in university years ago.

For the longest time, I could never see past his reputation. Mind you, he is highly successful today, but I kept seeing that "bad boy" from university.

However, something changed during our conversation. For the first time in years, I did not see this person for what I had always known him to be. I saw him in a different light – for who he is currently. It felt like a scale fell off my eyes, and my mind was suddenly expanded. That was when the Holy Spirit dropped the word "Evolution" in my spirit, and the passage 2 Corinthians 2:16 came to mind.

"So then, from now on, we have a new perspective that refuses to evaluate people merely by their outward appearances. For that's how we once viewed the Anointed One, but no longer do we see Him with limited human insight" 2 Corinthians 2:16 (TPT).

Many of us, like me, are fixated on the idea of how we view certain people or even the world, that our eyes and mind are shut to their current realities. People evolve, things change.

If you keep seeing people through the lenses of their past, chances are that you may miss out on what God is doing in their lives in the now. Chances are also that you are the one who needs to evolve.

One prayer that I have been praying lately is, "Lord, help me not to know men after the flesh, help me to see men as you see them" (2 Corinthians 2:16). I strongly believe that the scale falling off my eyes is is evidence of answered prayers. My mind is now expanded to the reality of people evolving.

If you keep seeing people through the lenses of their past, chances are that you may miss out on what God is doing in their lives in the now.

Many of us have missed out on opportunities and even helpers because we refuse to view people from the lenses of the present. **People evolve!!!**

KOFOWOROLA TORIOLA

love
notes

11

I am a call away- Holy Spirit

"But the Helper (Comforter, Advocate, Intercessor–Counselor, Strengthener, Standby), the Holy Spirit, whom the Father will send in My name [In My place, to represent Me and act on My behalf], He will teach you all things. And He will help you remember everything that I have told you."
John 14: 26 (AMP)

I am aware that grief is a very sensitive and touchy subject, so I shy away from discussing it. But I hope that if you are currently experiencing or even trying to wrap your head around how to deal with the loss of a loved one, that this little write up helps.

In 2020, a day before my dad's second year remembrance, I thought about my dad, and I could not process my feelings as I was trying to mentally prepare myself for his remembrance.

While at it, Asa's *"Eyé Àdabà"* dropped in my spirit. I was singing it mindlessly, but for some reason I could not move on from the song. While singing, it occurred to me that I didn't even know the meaning of Eyé Àdabà and I consulted google.

To my utmost surprise, it means a Dove. Immediately I sensed that this was not a random song pop up. The Holy Spirit was getting at something, so I proceeded to google the significance of a Dove. The first line that popped up was "The Holy Spirit". I could not believe that before my search, this did not even occur to me.

"Eyé Àdabà ti n fo loke wa bale mi ooo" (Dove, come and descend upon me)". This tied to the baptism of Jesus when the Holy Spirit descended upon Him like a dove.[xiii]

The Holy Spirit used a song to reveal – what I already knew but did not pay attention to – that He is right here and always will be regardless of my dad's passing.

He wanted to remind me that I can always rely on him and in those moments when I feel sad or unable to process my feelings, that He is only a "Holy Spirit, I need you" away.

I am sharing this with you, especially if you are nursing hurt from the loss of a loved one. I need you to know that Jesus did not leave you comfortless. He promised you a helper, comforter, advocate, intercessor, counselor and strengthener– a total package if you ask me – in the Holy Spirit.[xiv]

At that moment, when you feel helpless and maybe emotionally unbalanced, remember, He is only a "Holy Spirit, help me, I need you" away.

Jesus did not leave you comfortless. He promised you a helper, comforter, advocate, intercessor, counselor and strengthener– a total package if you ask me – in the Holy Spirit

Sending love and light to everyone grieving. I pray that the peace of God which passes all understanding floods your heart. I pray you find peace in the storm and certainty amid your uncertainty and above all, I pray that you are reassured of the love of God.

KOFOWOROLA TORIOLA

love notes

12

"When you have eaten and are satisfied, praise the Lord your God for the good land he has given you. Be careful that you do not forget the Lord your God, failing to observe his commands, his laws and his decrees that I am giving you this day."
Deut 8:10(NIV)

For the first time in my life, I realized in 2019 that I am privileged.

The degree, I cannot quantify, but privilege is privilege. Maybe I don't have a car or a house of my own or can't travel as often as I wish. Maybe I don't have 30 billion Naira in my account or even 3 million Naira but that does not negate the fact that to a large extent, I am privileged.

One fateful morning, the woman that helps with my laundry (imagine I even have someone that does my laundry) came over and because her phone was faulty, she couldn't call me when she got to the gate. She knocked but I didn't hear her. It was raining heavily so the doors and windows were shut.

She stood in the rain for what I guessed must have been about 2 hours before I opened the gate by sheer coincidence.

I could not help but think that those hours were the longest she had ever had to experience. While she stood in the rain, I slept in the comfort of my room. She was probably struggling with the idea of going back home. Who knows, what if her transport fare back home or her next meal or her children's was probably going to be from the money I would pay?

I felt terribly bad. How much was I even paying that would warrant her waiting in the rain for that long? The rain was quite heavy.

Whether I admit it or not, whether my bank balance agrees

or not, in one way or another, I am privileged as with many of us.

To be honest, God wanted to open my eyes to this reality because I had been complaining a lot about how things were not working out. I was getting angry at God and asking so many questions that I lost sight of things I termed "normal". But my normal is another person's prayer point. My it-is-one-of-those-things is another's answered prayers.

Like me, are you angry at God because things are not going the way you want? I hope this opens your eyes, like it did mine, to the realities of the faithfulness of God.

Pray with me

Lord, thank you for this revelation
I'm sorry for the things I've termed normal.
I'm sorry for taking your grace for granted.
I'm sorry for being too familiar and neglecting to reverence you.
Thank you for my little
Thank you for the good and bad times
Thank you for your love
Thank you for being mindful of me
Thank you for forgiving me

Amen!

TOFOWOROLA TORIOLA

love notes

13

25 Things every young wo(man) should know

"Teach us to number our days carefully so that we may develop wisdom in our hearts."
Psl 90:12(HCBS)

In 2018, I made what I like to term, "one of the greatest decisions in my life". I enrolled in a boot camp targeted at transforming lives and renewing minds, specifically for females. One of the topics during the boot camp was **"25 things every young woman should know".**

I did not realise how much this topic had characterized my life until recently when I picked up my notes from the boot camp.

I have replicated the lessons below and I can tell you for free that if you correctly apply these suggestions, you will be forever grateful. I am speaking from personal experience.

Be mindful that the lessons apply to everyone regardless of age and gender.

1. Be interested in things. Try to explore life, explore other states, learn a new language, join a club – book, travel, music etc.
2. It is okay to be you. Be confident, identify your values, build your belief system.

> ***Be Nice, Be Kind. Be firm but be nice. It always pays to be nice.***

3. Be Nice, Be Kind. Be firm but be nice. It always pays to be nice.
4. Never expect much from people. Just give, give and give some more.
5. Make friends. Start building your network, build your inner circle.
6. Learn to say No without feeling guilty. Say No on your own terms.

7. Enjoy your own company. Dine alone, take yourself out.
8. Be useful around the house.
9. Financial Literacy is key.
10. Have a life vision.
11. Confront your friends without losing them forever.
12. Exercise.
13. Read, Read, Read.
14. Learn to Sew (more like learn to stitch).
15. Work, Work, Work. Work with your brain and physical strength.
16. Stop trying to please people.
17. Do you!
18. Even if you don't like or know how to cook, just know how to make 3 meals.
19. Know when to apologise.
20. Find a mentor and don't take the relationship for granted.
21. Ask for help.
22. Look into the mirror and see the beauty you were born into.
23. Control your emotions.
24. Have your own political views.
25. Listen a lot and know when to speak.

Bonus

26. Don't be pressured by your peers, parents and public for overnight success.

27. Be intentional.
28. Know God and trust God.

Add your own recommendations to the list.

These are extremely useful lessons for everyone, and I implore you to have this non-exhaustive list at the back of your mind while navigating through life.

14

Do you believe in God?

"As they talked and discussed these things, Jesus Himself suddenly came and began walking with them. But God kept them from recognizing Him...as they sat down to eat, he took the bread and blessed it. Then he broke it and gave it to them. Suddenly, their eyes were opened, and they recognized Him. And at that moment He disappeared!"
Luke 24:14-15, 30-31

As we come to the end of this love notes series, I would like to invoke something in you about the nature and character of God.

Do you believe in God?

I believe that I'd get like an 80% yes.

Who is God to you?

I never have a definite answer to this because God proves himself to be different things in my life at different times and in different situations. But in 2020, he proved himself to be a "precise" God and an "attention to detail" kind of God.

I know these are not the typical names of God we know but hey! When has God ever been typical?

Let me share this weird story with you. Every time I remember it, I am more in awe of God.

One fateful Saturday evening, I just felt sort of "lonely", so I took myself out to cheer myself up. Not sure this decision helped. I had gone to get my comfort food – ice cream. Stepping into ColdStone store, you'd think it was Valentine's Day. I was like "get a room please". I bought my ice cream, sat at a corner and was just observing and admiring different couples across various age grades dining in there. While at it, I poured out my frustration to God and said, "I'd really like someone to keep me company, I feel lonely". It was not a prayer for a romantic relationship to be fair, I just did not feel like I had anyone to talk to at that moment.

I finished my ice cream and walked out. I had the option of

taking a bus or walking home. It was not a really long walk. Maybe about 20-30 minutes. So, I opted for a walk with the intention of listening to music and enjoying the evening breeze, just to clear my head.

Out of the blues, a guy walked up to me and started talking to me. I already rolled my eyes at this *bad belle** that was about to ruin my walk home, but I decided to give the conversation a chance. What's the worst that could happen? I will board a bus as an excuse if I need to escape the conversation.

Surprisingly, the conversation was so good, and we chatted like we had known each other all our lives. He was of the same age as my younger brother and they even had a lot in common. He walked me home and just left. I never gave thoughts to what happened that evening, but I knew that the "lonely" feeling disappeared and I felt some sort of warmth.

Fast forward to a few days later, the Holy Spirit reminded me about my prayer while indulging in my ice cream. Then it dawned on me that God sent him. I was mind blown and I could not explain the feeling. I just started screaming and crying. Since then, I have referred to God as "my attention to detail" kind of God. After that evening, I have experienced God in this dimension on occasions too numerous to share. That experience reminds me of Jesus' revelation of Himself to the men on the road to Emmaus.[xv] Jesus was right beside me, but I didn't realise until a few days later.

The Holy Spirit brought this to my remembrance again to remind me of who He is. It is His track record to tell me that He sees me, and He is paying attention to every detail of my life. I don't know whether God has revealed himself to you, but I'd like you to cast your mind on who God is to you as we wind down in this book.

In reflecting, cast your mind back to how examples of this revelation have occurred in your life. As you do this, it encourages you to judge Him faithful, stirs your faith and puts you in a position of thanksgiving.

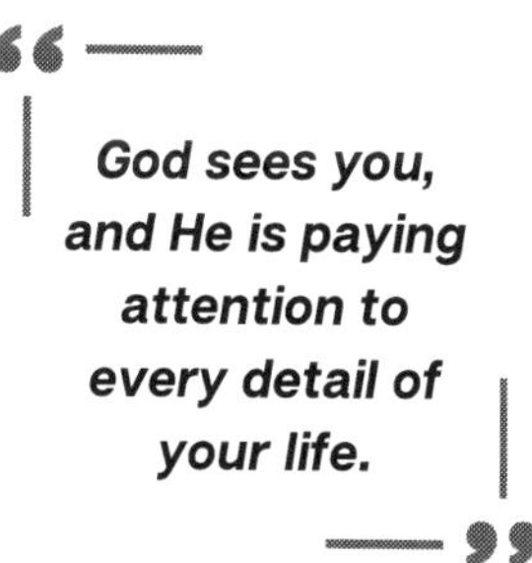

Afterword

When people ask why Love Notes? My obvious yet unlikely response is LOVE.

Love Notes is an expression of my love in form of sharing, sharing my experiences with hopes that it serves as a guide to others.

Sharing is an integral part of my life. I have learnt that in sharing, I communicate the power of togetherness. The truth is, many people are winging life; and sometimes the journey may seem lonely. Through sharing, people can relate to some of my experiences as they feel seen, loved, supported, and helped; thereby, reassuring them that they are not alone in the journey of life.

We are truly not called to do life alone. Through Love Notes, I have shared my journey with the readers in the most vulnerable manner while providing insights into some of my deepest conversations with God. Some notes were written from a place of pain, some on my knees in total surrender to God, some in tears and others from a place of gratitude. Regardless of how I felt, one thing was constant – God's love.

Afterword

Every day is an opportunity to introduce someone to the love of God. I want readers of Love Notes to experience a multidimension of God's love while navigating different phases of life – identity crises, emotional imbalance, grief and struggle with vulnerability.

I can't promise that Love Notes will answer all your burning questions about life, but I hope it takes you a step closer to finding the answer.

If you would like to take certain conversations in Love Notes further, please feel free to reach out to me on my social media platforms:

Instagram: @dearkofoworola
Twitter: @dearkofoworola

Affirmations

I

I am created by God, he designed me,
so, I am not a mistake
His son died for me so I can be forgiven
He picked me to be his own, so I'm chosen
He redeemed me, so I'm wanted
He showed me grace, just so I can be saved
He has a future for me because He loves me
I no longer wonder; I am a child of God [xvi]

II

I see myself the way God sees me
I am a reflection of my heavenly father and
I am made in His imagine
I trust in the Lord with all my heart and
Lean not on my own understanding
In all my ways, I will acknowledge God and
I will trust him to direct my path

III

God is redirecting my focus to my future
I will no longer be looking at things in my past
or around me
I receive an awesome revelation of my future

Affirmations

IV
Lord, please help me to be a Christian in my heart
Help me to live more Holy
Help me to imitate Jesus
Teach me that your grace is available to me and
That your strength is made perfect in my weakness

V
I am taking my thoughts and subjecting them to the obedience of Christ[xvii]
I can do all things through Christ who strengthens me, including taking control of my emotions

VI
I attract good and quality relationships
I enjoy the gifts of men and from men
God is strategically connecting me with purpose partners

VII
God is mindful of me and interested
in every detail of my life
God will not leave me stranded
God can be trusted. Therefore, I trust Him completely
His strength is made perfect in my weakness

Affirmations

VIII
God has given me the spirit of joy and gladness instead of grief
I will rejoice with my friends and family
Because I know God is in my neighbourhood
I rest in the confidence that my current circumstances do not define me

IX
I will focus on whatever is true,
whatever is honourable and worthy of respect,
whatever is right and confirmed by God's word,
whatever is pure and wholesome,
whatever is lovely and brings peace,
whatever is admirable and of good repute.
if there is any excellence,
if there is anything worthy of praise,
I will think continually on these things
[centre my mind on them,
and implant them in my heart][xvii]

X
I evolve
My mind is expanded in this season.

Affirmations

I begin to see people the way God sees them.
I receive an increased capacity to accurately discern the move of God in the life of a person per season.
The devil does not capitalize on my mindset to make you lose out on opportunities

Resources

I Overcomer. Directed by Alex Kendrick, Affirm Films, 2019, Netflix App, 4

ii Lexico (n.d.) Lexico.com dictionary retrieved 15 February, 2022 from https://www.lexico.com/definition/vision_board, 14

iii Habakkuk 2:2-3, New Living Translation, 14

iv Ephesians 1:17, Amplified Bible, 15

v Genesis 13:14-18, New International Version, 15

vi Habakkuk 2:2, New Living Translation, 16

vii Hebrews 11: 1, Living Bible, 17

viii *The Difference between Religion and Christianity* (2012) retrieved 15 February, 2022 from https://footsoldiers4christ.wordpress.com/2012/06/05/the-difference-between-religion-and-christianity/, 20

ix Joyce Meyers, (1997) *Managing Your Emotions*, 20

x Black's Law Dictionary, 26

xi Luke 11:33, 36

xii Priscilla Shier, *When it feels like God is doing nothing* [Video], YouTube https://youtu.be/6sjvCx2o76M, 39

xiii Matthew 3:1, 50

xiv John 14:26, Amplified Bible, 51

xv Luke 24:13-35, 64

xvi *Overcomer*, ibid, 67

xvii 2 Corinthians 10:5, 68

xviii Philippians 4:8, Amplified Bible, 69

xix Cindy Trim, (2018) *Hello Tomorrow! The Transformational Power of Vision*, Charisma Media

xx Immerse Coaching Inner Circle https://immerseinnercircle.com/

xxi Dr. James Dobson, (2012) *When God does not make sense: Holding on to your faith during the hardest time*, Tyndale House

* Ginger – to be catalyzed to do something
* Gas – to encourage
* Sọ̀rọ̀ sókè– to speak up
* God me nko – God what about me
* Bad belle – a person who has bad wishes for a person

Printed in Great Britain
by Amazon